41 Greece Restaurant Recipes for Home

By: Kelly Johnson

Table of Contents

- Moussaka
- Spanakopita
- Souvlaki
- Tzatziki
- Dolmadakia
- Avgolemono Soup
- Baklava
- Gyro
- Greek Salad
- Fasolada
- Gigantes Plaki
- Horiatiki (Village Salad)
- Kleftiko
- Briam
- Saganaki
- Tiropita
- Kavourmas (Pork Preserved in Lard)
- Kolokithokeftedes (Zucchini Fritters)
- Loukoumades (Honey Puffs)
- Pastitsio
- Soutzouk Loukoum
- Lentil Soup
- Kalitsounia (Cretan Cheese Pastries)
- Stifado
- Skordalia
- Htipiti (Feta and Pepper Dip)
- Kokkinisto (Beef in Tomato Sauce)
- Panzaria Me Skordalia (Beetroot Salad with Garlic Dip)
- Revithada (Chickpea Stew)
- Lahanosalata (Cabbage Salad)
- Pita with Spinach and Feta
- Feta Saganaki

- Megalokavourmas (Big Pork Roast)
- Bougatsa (Custard Pie)
- Mizithra Cheese Pasta
- Yemista (Stuffed Tomatoes and Peppers)
- Soutzouk Loukoum
- Greek Lamb Chops
- Baked Feta with Olives and Herbs
- Choriatiki (Greek Village Salad)
- Galaktoboureko

Moussaka

Ingredients:

- **For the Eggplant:**
    - 2 large eggplants
    - Olive oil
    - Salt
- **For the Meat Sauce:**
    - 1 lb (450g) ground beef or lamb
    - 1 large onion, chopped
    - 2 cloves garlic, minced
    - 1 can (14 oz) crushed tomatoes
    - 2 tbsp tomato paste
    - 1/2 cup red wine (optional)
    - 1 tsp ground cinnamon
    - 1/2 tsp ground allspice
    - 1 tsp dried oregano
    - Salt and pepper to taste
    - 2 tbsp olive oil
- **For the Béchamel Sauce:**
    - 4 tbsp butter
    - 1/4 cup all-purpose flour
    - 2 cups milk
    - 1/2 cup grated Parmesan cheese
    - 1/4 tsp ground nutmeg
    - Salt and pepper to taste
    - 1 large egg, beaten

Instructions:

1. **Prepare the Eggplant:**
    - Slice eggplants into 1/2-inch rounds. Sprinkle with salt and let sit for 30 minutes to draw out moisture. Rinse and pat dry.
    - Preheat oven to 400°F (200°C). Brush eggplant slices with olive oil and place on a baking sheet. Bake for 20 minutes, flipping halfway, until golden and tender.
2. **Prepare the Meat Sauce:**
    - Heat olive oil in a large skillet over medium heat. Add onion and garlic, and cook until softened.
    - Add ground meat and cook until browned. Drain excess fat if necessary.
    - Stir in crushed tomatoes, tomato paste, red wine (if using), cinnamon, allspice, oregano, salt, and pepper. Simmer for 20 minutes until thickened.
3. **Prepare the Béchamel Sauce:**

- Melt butter in a saucepan over medium heat. Stir in flour and cook for 1-2 minutes.
- Gradually whisk in milk, cooking until the mixture thickens and becomes smooth.
- Remove from heat and stir in Parmesan cheese, nutmeg, salt, pepper, and beaten egg. Mix until smooth.

4. **Assemble the Moussaka:**
    - Preheat oven to 375°F (190°C).
    - In a baking dish, layer half of the eggplant slices. Spread meat sauce evenly over the eggplant. Top with remaining eggplant slices.
    - Pour béchamel sauce over the top, spreading evenly.

5. **Bake:**
    - Bake for 45-50 minutes, or until the top is golden and bubbly. Allow to cool for 15 minutes before serving.

Enjoy your homemade moussaka!

Spanakopita

Ingredients:

- **For the Filling:**
    - 1 lb (450g) fresh spinach or 1 package frozen spinach (thawed and drained)
    - 1/2 cup chopped fresh parsley
    - 1/2 cup chopped fresh dill
    - 1 cup crumbled feta cheese
    - 1/2 cup ricotta cheese
    - 1/2 cup grated Parmesan cheese
    - 1 small onion, finely chopped
    - 2 cloves garlic, minced
    - 2 large eggs
    - Salt and pepper to taste
    - 2 tbsp olive oil
- **For the Assembly:**
    - 1 package phyllo dough (16 oz), thawed
    - 1/2 cup melted butter or olive oil

Instructions:

1. **Prepare the Filling:**
    - Heat olive oil in a large skillet over medium heat. Add onion and garlic, and cook until softened.
    - Stir in spinach and cook until wilted (if using fresh) or heated through (if using frozen). Remove from heat and let cool slightly.
    - In a large bowl, combine the cooked spinach mixture, parsley, dill, feta, ricotta, Parmesan, eggs, salt, and pepper. Mix well.
2. **Assemble the Spanakopita:**
    - Preheat oven to 375°F (190°C).
    - Brush a 9x13-inch baking dish with melted butter or olive oil.
    - Lay one sheet of phyllo dough in the dish and brush lightly with butter or oil. Repeat with 6-8 sheets, layering and brushing each with butter or oil.
    - Spread the spinach filling evenly over the phyllo layers.
    - Layer the remaining phyllo sheets over the filling, brushing each sheet with butter or oil. Use about 6-8 sheets for the top layer.
    - Trim any overhanging phyllo, tuck the edges into the dish, and brush the top with more melted butter or oil.
3. **Bake:**
    - Bake for 45-50 minutes, or until the top is golden brown and crispy.
    - Allow to cool slightly before cutting into squares or triangles.

Enjoy your Spanakopita!

Souvlaki

Ingredients:

- **For the Marinade:**
    - 1/2 cup olive oil
    - 1/4 cup lemon juice
    - 3 cloves garlic, minced
    - 2 tbsp dried oregano
    - 1 tsp dried thyme
    - 1 tsp paprika
    - 1/2 tsp ground cumin
    - Salt and pepper to taste
- **For the Souvlaki:**
    - 1 1/2 lbs (680g) boneless chicken thighs or pork tenderloin, cut into 1-inch cubes
    - Wooden or metal skewers (soaked if wooden)

Instructions:

1. **Prepare the Marinade:**
    - In a bowl, whisk together olive oil, lemon juice, garlic, oregano, thyme, paprika, cumin, salt, and pepper.
2. **Marinate the Meat:**
    - Place meat cubes in a large resealable bag or bowl. Pour marinade over the meat and toss to coat evenly.
    - Marinate in the refrigerator for at least 1 hour, preferably overnight.
3. **Grill the Souvlaki:**
    - Preheat grill to medium-high heat.
    - Thread marinated meat onto skewers.
    - Grill skewers for 8-12 minutes, turning occasionally, until the meat is cooked through and has nice grill marks.
4. **Serve:**
    - Serve the souvlaki with pita bread, tzatziki sauce, and your favorite vegetables.

Enjoy your delicious homemade Souvlaki!

Tzatziki

Ingredients:

- 1 cup Greek yogurt (full-fat or 2%)
- 1/2 cucumber, peeled, seeded, and grated
- 2 cloves garlic, minced
- 1 tbsp olive oil
- 1 tbsp fresh lemon juice (or 1-2 tsp white vinegar)
- 1 tbsp chopped fresh dill (or 1 tsp dried dill)
- Salt to taste
- Black pepper to taste

Instructions:

1. **Prepare the Cucumber:**
   - Grate the cucumber and place it in a fine mesh strainer. Sprinkle with a little salt and let it sit for about 10 minutes to release excess moisture.
   - After 10 minutes, squeeze the grated cucumber in a clean kitchen towel or paper towel to remove as much liquid as possible.
2. **Combine Ingredients:**
   - In a mixing bowl, combine Greek yogurt, grated cucumber, minced garlic, olive oil, lemon juice, and dill. Mix well.
3. **Season:**
   - Add salt and pepper to taste. Adjust seasoning as needed.
4. **Chill:**
   - Refrigerate for at least 1 hour to allow flavors to meld.
5. **Serve:**
   - Serve chilled as a dip with pita bread or as a sauce with grilled meats and vegetables.

Enjoy your homemade Tzatziki!

Dolmadakia

Ingredients:

- **For the Filling:**
    - 1 cup rice (short or medium grain)
    - 1/2 cup pine nuts
    - 1/2 cup chopped fresh parsley
    - 1/2 cup chopped fresh dill
    - 1/2 cup chopped onion
    - 1/2 cup currants or raisins
    - 1/4 cup olive oil
    - 1/2 tsp ground cinnamon
    - Salt and pepper to taste
- **For the Dolmadakia:**
    - 1 jar grape leaves (about 16 oz), drained and rinsed
    - 1/2 cup lemon juice (about 2 lemons)
    - 1 cup water or vegetable broth
    - Extra olive oil for drizzling

Instructions:

1. **Prepare the Filling:**
    - In a large skillet, heat olive oil over medium heat. Add onions and cook until softened.
    - Stir in rice and cook for 2 minutes until slightly translucent.
    - Add pine nuts, currants, parsley, dill, cinnamon, salt, and pepper. Cook for another 2 minutes.
    - Add 1 cup of water or broth. Bring to a boil, then reduce heat, cover, and simmer for 10-15 minutes until rice is tender and liquid is absorbed. Let the filling cool slightly.
2. **Prepare the Grape Leaves:**
    - If the grape leaves are not already prepared, blanch them in boiling water for 1-2 minutes to soften, then drain and let cool.
3. **Stuff the Grape Leaves:**
    - Lay a grape leaf flat on a cutting board, vein side up. Place a tablespoon of filling near the stem end of the leaf.
    - Fold the sides of the leaf over the filling, then roll it up tightly from the stem end to the tip. Repeat with remaining leaves and filling.
4. **Cook the Dolmadakia:**
    - In a large pot, arrange the stuffed grape leaves in a single layer. Place them seam side down to prevent unrolling.
    - Drizzle with a little olive oil and pour in lemon juice and water or broth.

- Place a plate or lid on top of the dolmadakia to keep them submerged and simmer gently over low heat for 30-40 minutes until tender.
5. **Serve:**
    - Allow the dolmadakia to cool slightly before serving. They can be served warm or at room temperature, often with a side of yogurt or tzatziki.

Enjoy your homemade Dolmadakia!

Avgolemono Soup

Ingredients:

- 1 whole chicken (about 3-4 lbs), cut into pieces
- 1 medium onion, chopped
- 2 carrots, peeled and chopped
- 2 celery stalks, chopped
- 2 cloves garlic, minced
- 6 cups chicken broth
- 1 cup orzo or rice
- 3 large eggs
- 1/4 cup fresh lemon juice (about 2 lemons)
- Salt and pepper to taste
- Fresh dill or parsley for garnish (optional)

Instructions:

1. **Prepare the Broth:**
   - In a large pot, place the chicken pieces, onion, carrots, celery, and garlic. Cover with chicken broth and bring to a boil.
   - Reduce heat and simmer for 45 minutes to 1 hour, until the chicken is cooked through and the vegetables are tender.
2. **Remove the Chicken:**
   - Remove the chicken pieces from the pot and set aside to cool. Strain the broth if desired, then return it to the pot.
3. **Cook the Orzo/Rice:**
   - Add orzo or rice to the pot and cook according to package instructions until tender.
4. **Prepare the Avgolemono Mixture:**
   - In a bowl, whisk together the eggs and lemon juice until well combined.
5. **Temper the Egg Mixture:**
   - Slowly ladle a few cups of hot broth into the egg-lemon mixture, whisking constantly to temper the eggs and prevent curdling.
6. **Combine and Heat:**
   - Gradually stir the tempered egg mixture back into the pot of soup. Heat gently over low heat, stirring constantly, until the soup thickens slightly but do not allow it to boil.
7. **Shred and Add Chicken:**
   - While the soup is heating, shred the chicken meat from the bones and return it to the pot. Season with salt and pepper to taste.
8. **Serve:**
   - Garnish with fresh dill or parsley if desired. Serve warm.

Enjoy your creamy and tangy Avgolemono Soup!

Baklava

Ingredients:

- **For the Baklava:**
    - 1 package phyllo dough (16 oz), thawed
    - 1 1/2 cups unsalted butter, melted
    - 2 cups nuts (such as walnuts, pistachios, or almonds), finely chopped
    - 1 cup granulated sugar
    - 1 tsp ground cinnamon
- **For the Syrup:**
    - 1 cup granulated sugar
    - 1 cup water
    - 1/2 cup honey
    - 1 tsp vanilla extract
    - 1/2 tsp lemon juice

Instructions:

1. **Prepare the Nuts:**
    - In a bowl, combine chopped nuts, sugar, and cinnamon. Set aside.
2. **Prepare the Phyllo Dough:**
    - Preheat your oven to 350°F (175°C).
    - Brush a 9x13-inch baking dish with melted butter.
    - Lay one sheet of phyllo dough in the dish and brush with melted butter. Repeat this process, layering and buttering each sheet, until you have about 8 sheets layered.
3. **Add the Nut Filling:**
    - Sprinkle a thin layer of the nut mixture over the phyllo dough.
4. **Continue Layering:**
    - Continue layering phyllo sheets, brushing each with melted butter, and adding nut mixture every 5-6 sheets. Finish with about 8 sheets of phyllo on top, buttering each layer.
5. **Cut the Baklava:**
    - Using a sharp knife, cut the baklava into diamond or square shapes.
6. **Bake:**
    - Bake for 50-60 minutes, or until the baklava is golden brown and crisp.
7. **Prepare the Syrup:**
    - While the baklava is baking, make the syrup. In a saucepan, combine sugar, water, honey, and lemon juice. Bring to a boil, then reduce heat and simmer for about 10 minutes. Remove from heat and stir in vanilla extract.
8. **Pour Syrup:**

- Once the baklava is baked, remove it from the oven and immediately pour the hot syrup evenly over the baklava. Allow the baklava to cool completely and absorb the syrup before serving.

Enjoy your homemade Baklava!

Gyro

Ingredients:

- **For the Gyro Meat:**
    - 1 lb (450g) ground lamb
    - 1 lb (450g) ground beef
    - 1/2 cup finely chopped onion
    - 3 cloves garlic, minced
    - 1 tbsp dried oregano
    - 1 tbsp ground cumin
    - 1 tsp smoked paprika
    - 1 tsp ground coriander
    - 1/2 tsp ground cinnamon
    - Salt and pepper to taste
- **For the Tzatziki Sauce:**
    - 1 cup Greek yogurt
    - 1/2 cucumber, peeled, seeded, and grated
    - 2 cloves garlic, minced
    - 1 tbsp olive oil
    - 1 tbsp fresh lemon juice
    - 1 tbsp chopped fresh dill
    - Salt and pepper to taste
- **To Serve:**
    - Pita bread or flatbreads
    - Sliced tomatoes
    - Sliced onions
    - Shredded lettuce

Instructions:

1. **Prepare the Gyro Meat:**
    - Preheat oven to 375°F (190°C).
    - In a bowl, mix together ground lamb, ground beef, onion, garlic, oregano, cumin, paprika, coriander, cinnamon, salt, and pepper until well combined.
    - Form the mixture into a loaf shape and place it on a baking sheet or in a loaf pan.
    - Bake for 45-60 minutes, or until the meat is cooked through and reaches an internal temperature of 160°F (71°C).
2. **Prepare the Tzatziki Sauce:**
    - In a bowl, combine Greek yogurt, grated cucumber (squeezed to remove excess moisture), garlic, olive oil, lemon juice, dill, salt, and pepper. Mix well and refrigerate until ready to use.
3. **Slice the Gyro Meat:**

- Once the meat is cooked, let it rest for 10 minutes before slicing thinly against the grain.
4. **Assemble the Gyros:**
     - Warm the pita bread in a dry skillet or oven.
     - Spread tzatziki sauce on the pita, top with sliced gyro meat, and add tomatoes, onions, and lettuce.
5. **Serve:**
     - Serve the gyros wrapped or open-faced with additional tzatziki sauce on the side.

Enjoy your homemade Gyro!

Greek Salad

Ingredients:

- 3 cups cherry tomatoes, halved
- 1 cucumber, peeled and sliced
- 1/2 red onion, thinly sliced
- 1/2 cup Kalamata olives, pitted
- 1/2 cup feta cheese, crumbled or in chunks
- 1/4 cup extra-virgin olive oil
- 2 tbsp red wine vinegar
- 1 tsp dried oregano
- Salt and black pepper to taste
- Fresh parsley for garnish (optional)

Instructions:

1. **Combine Vegetables:**
    - In a large bowl, combine cherry tomatoes, cucumber, red onion, and olives.
2. **Add Feta:**
    - Gently mix in the feta cheese.
3. **Prepare the Dressing:**
    - In a small bowl or jar, whisk together olive oil, red wine vinegar, oregano, salt, and pepper.
4. **Dress the Salad:**
    - Pour the dressing over the salad and toss gently to combine.
5. **Garnish and Serve:**
    - Garnish with fresh parsley if desired. Serve immediately or chill until ready to serve.

Enjoy your refreshing Greek Salad!

Fasolada

Ingredients:

- 1 cup dried white beans (such as cannellini or navy), soaked overnight
- 1/4 cup olive oil
- 1 onion, chopped
- 2 carrots, peeled and chopped
- 2 celery stalks, chopped
- 3 cloves garlic, minced
- 1 can (14 oz) crushed tomatoes
- 1 tbsp tomato paste
- 1 tsp dried oregano
- 1/2 tsp dried thyme
- 1 bay leaf
- 6 cups vegetable or chicken broth
- 1/4 cup fresh parsley, chopped
- Salt and pepper to taste

Instructions:

1. **Prepare the Beans:**
    - Drain and rinse the soaked beans. Set aside.
2. **Cook the Vegetables:**
    - In a large pot, heat olive oil over medium heat. Add onion, carrots, and celery, and cook until softened, about 5-7 minutes.
    - Stir in garlic and cook for an additional minute.
3. **Add Beans and Tomatoes:**
    - Add the beans, crushed tomatoes, tomato paste, oregano, thyme, bay leaf, and broth. Bring to a boil.
4. **Simmer:**
    - Reduce heat, cover, and simmer for 1 to 1.5 hours, or until beans are tender. Stir occasionally and add more broth if necessary.
5. **Season and Finish:**
    - Remove the bay leaf. Stir in fresh parsley and season with salt and pepper to taste.
6. **Serve:**
    - Serve hot, drizzled with extra olive oil if desired.

Enjoy your hearty and nutritious Fasolada!

Gigantes Plaki

Ingredients:

- 1 cup dried gigante beans (or substitute with large white beans)
- 1/4 cup olive oil
- 1 large onion, chopped
- 3 cloves garlic, minced
- 1 red bell pepper, chopped
- 1 can (14 oz) crushed tomatoes
- 2 tbsp tomato paste
- 1 tsp dried oregano
- 1/2 tsp dried thyme
- 1 bay leaf
- 1/4 cup fresh parsley, chopped
- 1/2 tsp sugar (optional)
- Salt and pepper to taste

Instructions:

1. **Prepare the Beans:**
   - Soak the dried beans overnight in plenty of water. Drain and rinse.
   - Cook the beans in a large pot of boiling water for 45-60 minutes, or until tender. Drain and set aside.
2. **Prepare the Sauce:**
   - In a large skillet or saucepan, heat olive oil over medium heat. Add onion and cook until softened, about 5 minutes.
   - Stir in garlic and red bell pepper, and cook for another 2 minutes.
   - Add crushed tomatoes, tomato paste, oregano, thyme, bay leaf, and sugar (if using). Simmer for 10 minutes, allowing the flavors to meld.
3. **Combine Beans and Sauce:**
   - Preheat oven to 375°F (190°C).
   - In a large baking dish, combine the cooked beans with the tomato sauce. Stir in fresh parsley and season with salt and pepper.
4. **Bake:**
   - Cover the baking dish with aluminum foil and bake for 30-40 minutes, or until the beans are tender and the sauce has thickened.
5. **Serve:**
   - Allow to cool slightly before serving. This dish can be enjoyed warm or at room temperature.

Enjoy your delicious Gigantes Plaki!

Horiatiki (Village Salad)

Ingredients:

- 3-4 medium ripe tomatoes, cut into wedges
- 1 cucumber, peeled (if thick-skinned) and sliced or cut into chunks
- 1/2 red onion, thinly sliced
- 1/2 cup Kalamata olives, pitted
- 1/2 cup crumbled feta cheese (or feta in blocks)
- 1/4 cup extra-virgin olive oil
- 2 tbsp red wine vinegar (or fresh lemon juice)
- 1 tsp dried oregano
- Salt and black pepper to taste

Instructions:

1. **Prepare the Vegetables:**
   - In a large bowl, combine tomatoes, cucumber, red onion, and olives.
2. **Add Feta Cheese:**
   - Top the salad with crumbled or block feta cheese.
3. **Prepare the Dressing:**
   - In a small bowl, whisk together olive oil, red wine vinegar (or lemon juice), oregano, salt, and pepper.
4. **Dress the Salad:**
   - Drizzle the dressing over the salad and toss gently to combine, or leave the salad undisturbed and drizzle dressing over the top for a more rustic presentation.
5. **Serve:**
   - Serve immediately or let the salad sit for 15-20 minutes to allow flavors to meld.

Enjoy your fresh and tangy Horiatiki!

Kleftiko

Ingredients:

- 4-5 lbs (1.8-2.3 kg) lamb shoulder, cut into large chunks
- 1/4 cup olive oil
- 1 large onion, chopped
- 4 cloves garlic, minced
- 3-4 medium potatoes, peeled and cut into chunks
- 2 large carrots, peeled and sliced
- 1 red bell pepper, chopped
- 1 cup dry white wine or water
- 1 can (14 oz) crushed tomatoes
- 2 tbsp tomato paste
- 1 tbsp dried oregano
- 1 tsp dried rosemary
- 1 tsp dried thyme
- 1 bay leaf
- Salt and black pepper to taste
- Fresh lemon juice (optional, for serving)
- Fresh parsley, chopped (for garnish)

Instructions:

1. **Preheat Oven:**
   - Preheat your oven to 325°F (160°C).
2. **Prepare the Meat:**
   - In a large, oven-safe pot or Dutch oven, heat olive oil over medium-high heat.
   - Add lamb chunks and brown on all sides. Remove the lamb from the pot and set aside.
3. **Cook the Vegetables:**
   - In the same pot, add onion and cook until softened, about 5 minutes.
   - Stir in garlic and cook for an additional minute.
4. **Combine Ingredients:**
   - Return the browned lamb to the pot.
   - Add potatoes, carrots, and red bell pepper.
   - Pour in white wine or water, crushed tomatoes, and tomato paste.
   - Stir in oregano, rosemary, thyme, bay leaf, salt, and pepper.
5. **Bake:**
   - Cover the pot with a lid or aluminum foil.
   - Transfer to the oven and bake for 2.5 to 3 hours, or until the lamb is tender and the meat falls off the bone.
6. **Finish and Serve:**
   - If desired, drizzle with fresh lemon juice before serving.

- - Garnish with chopped parsley.

Serve your Kleftiko hot, ideally with crusty bread or over a bed of rice. Enjoy this flavorful and hearty Greek dish!

Briam

Ingredients:

- 2 large potatoes, peeled and sliced
- 2 zucchinis, sliced
- 1 large onion, chopped
- 1 red bell pepper, sliced
- 1 yellow bell pepper, sliced
- 1 eggplant, sliced
- 4-5 ripe tomatoes, chopped, or 1 can (14 oz) diced tomatoes
- 1/4 cup extra-virgin olive oil
- 3 cloves garlic, minced
- 1 tsp dried oregano
- 1/2 tsp dried thyme
- 1/2 tsp dried rosemary (optional)
- Salt and black pepper to taste
- Fresh parsley, chopped (for garnish)

Instructions:

1. **Preheat Oven:**
   - Preheat your oven to 400°F (200°C).
2. **Prepare the Vegetables:**
   - In a large bowl, combine potatoes, zucchinis, onion, bell peppers, and eggplant.
3. **Make the Sauce:**
   - In a separate bowl, mix chopped tomatoes (or canned tomatoes), olive oil, garlic, oregano, thyme, rosemary (if using), salt, and pepper.
4. **Combine and Roast:**
   - Pour the tomato mixture over the vegetables and toss to coat evenly.
   - Transfer the vegetables and sauce to a large baking dish or sheet pan.
5. **Bake:**
   - Cover the dish with aluminum foil and bake for 45 minutes.
   - Remove the foil and bake for an additional 15-20 minutes, or until the vegetables are tender and slightly caramelized.
6. **Garnish and Serve:**
   - Garnish with chopped parsley before serving.

Enjoy your flavorful and healthy Briam!

Saganaki

Ingredients:

- 8 oz (225g) kasseri cheese, halloumi, or any firm cheese suitable for frying (such as feta or mozzarella)
- 1/2 cup all-purpose flour
- 1 large egg, beaten
- 1/2 cup breadcrumbs (preferably panko for extra crunch)
- Olive oil or vegetable oil, for frying
- Lemon wedges, for serving
- Fresh parsley, chopped (optional, for garnish)

Instructions:

1. **Prepare the Cheese:**
   - Slice the cheese into 1/2-inch thick slices.
2. **Bread the Cheese:**
   - Place flour in a shallow dish.
   - Place beaten egg in another shallow dish.
   - Place breadcrumbs in a third shallow dish.
   - Dredge each cheese slice in flour, shaking off excess.
   - Dip into beaten egg, allowing excess to drip off.
   - Coat with breadcrumbs, pressing gently to adhere.
3. **Heat the Oil:**
   - Heat a generous amount of oil in a non-stick skillet over medium-high heat. You want enough oil to cover the bottom of the pan and come halfway up the sides of the cheese slices.
4. **Fry the Cheese:**
   - Fry cheese slices in batches (don't overcrowd the pan) for about 2-3 minutes per side, or until golden brown and crispy.
   - Remove from the pan and drain on paper towels.
5. **Serve:**
   - Serve hot with lemon wedges for squeezing over the cheese.
   - Garnish with fresh parsley if desired.

Enjoy your crispy and delicious Saganaki!

Tiropita

Ingredients:

- **For the Filling:**
    - 1 cup ricotta cheese
    - 1 cup feta cheese, crumbled
    - 1 cup grated mozzarella cheese (optional for extra creaminess)
    - 2 large eggs
    - 1/4 cup fresh parsley, chopped
    - 1/4 cup fresh dill, chopped (or 1 tsp dried dill)
    - Salt and black pepper to taste
- **For the Assembly:**
    - 1 package phyllo dough (16 oz), thawed
    - 1/2 cup unsalted butter or olive oil, melted
    - 1 egg (for egg wash, optional)

Instructions:

1. **Prepare the Filling:**
    - In a large bowl, combine ricotta cheese, feta cheese, mozzarella (if using), eggs, parsley, dill, salt, and pepper. Mix until well combined.
2. **Prepare the Phyllo Dough:**
    - Preheat your oven to 375°F (190°C).
    - Brush a 9x13-inch baking dish or a similar-sized oven-safe dish with melted butter or olive oil.
    - Lay one sheet of phyllo dough in the dish and brush lightly with melted butter or oil. Repeat this process, layering and buttering each sheet, until you have about 8 sheets layered.
3. **Add the Filling:**
    - Spread the cheese mixture evenly over the phyllo layers.
4. **Top the Pie:**
    - Continue layering with phyllo dough, brushing each sheet with melted butter or oil, until you have about 6-8 sheets layered on top.
    - Trim any excess phyllo, tuck the edges into the dish, and brush the top with more melted butter or oil.
    - Optionally, beat the remaining egg and brush over the top of the pie for a golden finish.
5. **Bake:**
    - Bake for 40-50 minutes, or until the top is golden brown and crispy.
6. **Cool and Serve:**
    - Allow the Tiropita to cool slightly before cutting into squares or triangles.

Enjoy your delicious Tiropita warm or at room temperature!

Kavourmas (Pork Preserved in Lard)

Ingredients:

- 3 lbs (1.4 kg) pork shoulder, cut into 1-inch cubes
- 1 lb (450g) pork belly, cut into 1-inch cubes
- 2 cups lard (or substitute with vegetable oil if necessary)
- 1 large onion, chopped
- 4 cloves garlic, minced
- 2 tbsp dried oregano
- 2 tsp paprika
- 1 tsp dried thyme
- 1 tsp ground black pepper
- 1 tsp salt
- 2 bay leaves
- 1 cup white wine (optional)

Instructions:

1. **Prepare the Meat:**
   - In a large bowl, combine pork shoulder and pork belly cubes. Season with salt, pepper, oregano, paprika, and thyme. Mix well to coat the meat evenly.
2. **Cook the Meat:**
   - In a large heavy-bottomed pot or Dutch oven, heat lard over medium heat until melted.
   - Add onions and cook until softened, about 5 minutes. Stir in garlic and cook for an additional minute.
   - Add the seasoned pork cubes to the pot. Cook, stirring occasionally, until the meat is browned on all sides.
3. **Add Liquids and Simmer:**
   - If using, pour in white wine and bring to a simmer. Cook for about 10 minutes until slightly reduced.
   - Add bay leaves and enough additional lard to completely cover the meat. The meat should be fully submerged in the fat.
4. **Preserve:**
   - Reduce heat to low. Cover and simmer gently for 1.5 to 2 hours, or until the meat is tender and the fat has rendered.
5. **Cool and Store:**
   - Allow the Kavourmas to cool to room temperature. Transfer the meat and fat into sterilized jars or containers. Ensure the meat is covered with fat to preserve it.
   - Store in the refrigerator for up to several weeks or in the freezer for longer storage.

Enjoy your Kavourmas as a flavorful preserved meat or as part of various dishes!

Kolokithokeftedes (Zucchini Fritters)

Ingredients:

- 4 medium zucchinis, grated
- 1 tsp salt
- 1 cup crumbled feta cheese
- 1/2 cup fresh mint, chopped (or 1/4 cup dried mint)
- 1/4 cup fresh parsley, chopped
- 1/2 cup finely chopped onion or green onions
- 2 large eggs
- 1/2 cup all-purpose flour
- 1/4 cup breadcrumbs (optional, for extra crispness)
- 1/2 tsp black pepper
- 1/2 tsp dried oregano (optional)
- Olive oil, for frying

Instructions:

1. **Prepare the Zucchini:**
    - Grate the zucchinis and place them in a colander. Sprinkle with salt and let sit for about 10 minutes to draw out excess moisture.
    - After 10 minutes, squeeze the grated zucchini with your hands or in a clean kitchen towel to remove as much liquid as possible.
2. **Mix the Ingredients:**
    - In a large bowl, combine the squeezed zucchini, crumbled feta cheese, mint, parsley, onion or green onions, eggs, flour, breadcrumbs (if using), black pepper, and oregano (if using). Mix well until everything is evenly incorporated.
3. **Heat the Oil:**
    - Heat a generous amount of olive oil in a large skillet over medium-high heat.
4. **Fry the Fritters:**
    - Drop spoonfuls of the zucchini mixture into the hot oil, flattening them slightly with the back of the spoon to form small patties.
    - Fry the fritters in batches, without overcrowding the pan, for about 2-3 minutes per side, or until golden brown and crispy.
5. **Drain and Serve:**
    - Remove the fritters from the skillet and drain on paper towels to remove excess oil.
    - Serve warm with a side of tzatziki or yogurt dip.

Enjoy your crispy and flavorful Kolokithokeftedes!

Loukoumades (Honey Puffs)

Ingredients:

- **For the Dough:**
    - 2 1/4 tsp active dry yeast (1 packet)
    - 1 1/2 cups warm water (110°F/45°C)
    - 1/4 cup granulated sugar
    - 1/4 cup plain Greek yogurt
    - 1/2 tsp salt
    - 3 cups all-purpose flour
- **For the Syrup:**
    - 1 cup granulated sugar
    - 1/2 cup honey
    - 1 cup water
    - 1 tsp lemon juice
    - 1 cinnamon stick (optional)
- **For Frying:**
    - Vegetable oil, for deep frying
- **For Garnish:**
    - Ground cinnamon (optional)
    - Chopped walnuts or sesame seeds (optional)

Instructions:

1. **Prepare the Dough:**
    - In a large bowl, dissolve the yeast and sugar in warm water. Let sit for about 5-10 minutes, or until frothy.
    - Add Greek yogurt, salt, and flour to the yeast mixture. Mix until a smooth, sticky dough forms.
    - Cover the bowl with a damp cloth and let the dough rise in a warm place for 1-1.5 hours, or until doubled in size.
2. **Prepare the Syrup:**
    - In a saucepan, combine sugar, honey, water, and lemon juice. Add the cinnamon stick if using.
    - Bring to a boil, then reduce heat and simmer for about 10 minutes, or until slightly thickened.
    - Remove from heat and let cool.
3. **Heat the Oil:**
    - In a large, deep skillet or pot, heat enough vegetable oil to cover the dough puffs, about 2-3 inches deep. Heat the oil to 350°F (175°C).
4. **Fry the Loukoumades:**
    - Using a spoon or cookie scoop, carefully drop spoonfuls of dough into the hot oil. Fry in batches, making sure not to overcrowd the pan.
    - Fry for 2-3 minutes per side, or until golden brown and puffed up.
    - Remove with a slotted spoon and drain on paper towels.
5. **Coat with Syrup:**

- While still warm, dip the loukoumades into the cooled syrup, or drizzle the syrup over them.
6. **Garnish and Serve:**
    - Optionally, sprinkle with ground cinnamon and chopped walnuts or sesame seeds.

Enjoy your sweet and sticky Loukoumades!

Pastitsio

Ingredients:

- **For the Meat Sauce:**
    - 2 tbsp olive oil
    - 1 onion, chopped
    - 3 cloves garlic, minced
    - 1 lb (450g) ground beef or lamb
    - 1 can (14 oz) crushed tomatoes
    - 2 tbsp tomato paste
    - 1/2 cup red wine (optional)
    - 1 tsp dried oregano
    - 1/2 tsp ground cinnamon
    - 1 bay leaf
    - Salt and pepper to taste
- **For the Pasta:**
    - 1 lb (450g) pasta (penne or macaroni works well)
    - 1 tbsp olive oil
    - 1/2 cup grated Parmesan cheese
- **For the Bechamel Sauce:**
    - 4 tbsp unsalted butter
    - 1/4 cup all-purpose flour
    - 2 cups milk
    - 1/2 tsp ground nutmeg
    - 1/2 cup grated Parmesan cheese
    - 1 egg, beaten

Instructions:

1. **Prepare the Meat Sauce:**
    - Heat olive oil in a large skillet over medium heat. Add onion and cook until softened, about 5 minutes.
    - Stir in garlic and cook for an additional minute.
    - Add ground beef or lamb and cook until browned. Drain excess fat if necessary.
    - Stir in crushed tomatoes, tomato paste, red wine (if using), oregano, cinnamon, and bay leaf. Simmer for 20-30 minutes, until thickened. Season with salt and pepper. Remove bay leaf.
2. **Cook the Pasta:**
    - Preheat your oven to 350°F (175°C).
    - Cook pasta according to package instructions until al dente. Drain and toss with 1 tbsp olive oil.
3. **Prepare the Bechamel Sauce:**

- In a saucepan, melt butter over medium heat. Stir in flour and cook for 1-2 minutes until lightly golden.
- Gradually whisk in milk and cook until the sauce thickens, about 5 minutes.
- Remove from heat and stir in nutmeg, Parmesan cheese, and beaten egg. Mix well.

4. **Assemble the Pastitsio:**
   - In a greased 9x13-inch baking dish, spread half of the cooked pasta. Top with the meat sauce, then the remaining pasta.
   - Pour the bechamel sauce over the top and smooth it out with a spatula. Sprinkle with extra Parmesan cheese if desired.

5. **Bake:**
   - Bake in the preheated oven for 30-40 minutes, until the top is golden brown and the dish is heated through.

6. **Cool and Serve:**
   - Let the Pastitsio cool for about 10 minutes before cutting into squares.

Enjoy your comforting and delicious Pastitsio!

Soutzouk Loukoum

Ingredients:

- 2 cups granulated sugar
- 1 cup water
- 1/2 cup cornstarch
- 1/4 cup rose water (or orange blossom water)
- 1/2 cup chopped walnuts or pistachios (optional)
- 1/2 cup powdered sugar, for dusting
- 1/4 cup cornstarch, for dusting

Instructions:

1. **Prepare the Mixture:**
    - In a medium saucepan, combine granulated sugar and water. Bring to a boil over medium heat, stirring until the sugar dissolves.
    - In a separate bowl, mix 1/2 cup cornstarch with 1 cup water to make a slurry. Gradually add this to the boiling sugar mixture, stirring continuously.
2. **Cook the Mixture:**
    - Reduce heat to low and cook the mixture, stirring constantly, for about 20-30 minutes, or until it thickens and becomes translucent.
3. **Add Flavor and Nuts:**
    - Stir in the rose water (or orange blossom water) and chopped nuts if using. Mix well.
4. **Set the Mixture:**
    - Pour the mixture into a greased or parchment-lined 8x8-inch pan. Smooth the surface with a spatula.
    - Let it set at room temperature for at least 4 hours, or until firm.
5. **Cut and Dust:**
    - Once set, dust a cutting board with a mixture of powdered sugar and cornstarch.
    - Turn the Soutzouk Loukoum out onto the dusted board and cut into small squares.
    - Dust the cut pieces with additional powdered sugar and cornstarch to prevent sticking.

Enjoy your homemade Soutzouk Loukoum as a sweet treat or gift!

Lentil Soup

Ingredients:

- **For the Soup:**
    - 1 cup dried green or brown lentils, rinsed
    - 1 large onion, chopped
    - 2 carrots, peeled and chopped
    - 2 celery stalks, chopped
    - 3 cloves garlic, minced
    - 1 can (14 oz) diced tomatoes
    - 6 cups vegetable or chicken broth
    - 1 bay leaf
    - 1 tsp ground cumin
    - 1/2 tsp dried thyme
    - 1/2 tsp paprika
    - Salt and black pepper to taste
    - 2 tbsp olive oil
- **For Garnish (Optional):**
    - Fresh parsley, chopped
    - Lemon wedges

Instructions:

1. **Prepare the Vegetables:**
    - Heat olive oil in a large pot over medium heat.
    - Add the chopped onion, carrots, and celery. Cook until the vegetables are softened, about 5-7 minutes.
    - Stir in the garlic and cook for an additional 1 minute.
2. **Add Lentils and Broth:**
    - Add the rinsed lentils, diced tomatoes, vegetable or chicken broth, bay leaf, cumin, thyme, and paprika to the pot.
    - Bring the mixture to a boil.
3. **Simmer the Soup:**
    - Reduce the heat to low, cover, and simmer for about 30-40 minutes, or until the lentils are tender.
4. **Season and Serve:**
    - Remove the bay leaf.
    - Season with salt and black pepper to taste.
    - Optionally, garnish with fresh parsley and serve with lemon wedges on the side for a fresh, zesty flavor.

Enjoy your hearty and nutritious Lentil Soup!

Kalitsounia (Cretan Cheese Pastries)

Ingredients:

- **For the Dough:**
    - 2 cups all-purpose flour
    - 1/2 cup unsalted butter, cold and cut into small pieces
    - 1/4 cup granulated sugar
    - 1/4 cup plain Greek yogurt
    - 1 large egg
    - 1/2 tsp baking powder
    - 1/4 tsp salt
- **For the Filling:**
    - 1 cup ricotta cheese
    - 1/2 cup crumbled feta cheese
    - 1/4 cup fresh mint, chopped (or 1 tbsp dried mint)
    - 1/4 cup fresh parsley, chopped
    - 1 large egg
    - 1 tbsp honey (optional, for sweetness)
    - Salt and black pepper to taste
- **For Baking:**
    - 1 egg, beaten (for egg wash)
    - Sesame seeds or poppy seeds (optional, for topping)

Instructions:

1. **Prepare the Dough:**
    - In a large bowl, mix flour, sugar, and salt. Cut in cold butter using a pastry cutter or your fingers until the mixture resembles coarse crumbs.
    - In a separate bowl, whisk together yogurt and egg. Add to the flour mixture and mix until a dough forms. Knead briefly on a floured surface until smooth.
    - Wrap the dough in plastic wrap and refrigerate for 30 minutes.
2. **Prepare the Filling:**
    - In a bowl, combine ricotta cheese, feta cheese, mint, parsley, egg, and honey (if using). Mix well and season with salt and pepper.
3. **Assemble the Pastries:**
    - Preheat your oven to 375°F (190°C) and line a baking sheet with parchment paper.
    - Roll out the dough on a floured surface to about 1/8 inch thickness. Cut into circles using a cookie cutter or glass (about 3 inches in diameter).
    - Place a spoonful of filling in the center of each dough circle. Fold the dough over to form a half-moon shape and press the edges to seal. You can also use a fork to crimp the edges.

4. **Bake:**
    - Place the filled pastries on the prepared baking sheet. Brush with beaten egg and sprinkle with sesame seeds or poppy seeds if desired.
    - Bake for 20-25 minutes, or until golden brown.
5. **Cool and Serve:**
    - Allow the pastries to cool slightly before serving.

Enjoy your delicious Kalitsounia warm or at room temperature!

Stifado

Ingredients:

- 2 lbs (900g) beef stew meat, cut into chunks
- 1/4 cup olive oil
- 2 large onions, chopped
- 4 cloves garlic, minced
- 1/4 cup tomato paste
- 1 can (14 oz) crushed tomatoes
- 1 cup red wine (optional)
- 1 cup beef broth
- 2 bay leaves
- 1 tsp dried oregano
- 1/2 tsp ground cinnamon
- 1/4 tsp ground cloves
- 1/4 cup fresh parsley, chopped
- 1 lb (450g) small pearl onions or shallots, peeled
- Salt and black pepper to taste

Instructions:

1. **Brown the Meat:**
   - Heat olive oil in a large pot or Dutch oven over medium-high heat.
   - Add beef chunks and brown on all sides. Remove the beef and set aside.
2. **Cook the Onions:**
   - In the same pot, add chopped onions and cook until softened, about 5 minutes.
   - Stir in garlic and cook for another minute.
3. **Add the Tomato Paste:**
   - Stir in tomato paste and cook for 2 minutes, until slightly caramelized.
4. **Combine Ingredients:**
   - Return the beef to the pot. Add crushed tomatoes, red wine (if using), beef broth, bay leaves, oregano, cinnamon, cloves, and parsley.
   - Season with salt and pepper.
5. **Simmer:**
   - Bring to a boil, then reduce heat to low. Cover and simmer for 1.5 to 2 hours, or until the beef is tender.
6. **Add Onions:**
   - Add the small pearl onions or shallots to the pot. Continue to cook for another 30 minutes, or until the onions are tender and the stew has thickened.
7. **Serve:**
   - Remove bay leaves before serving. Garnish with additional chopped parsley if desired.

Enjoy your rich and hearty Stifado!

Skordalia

Ingredients:

- 4-5 large cloves garlic, minced
- 2 cups day-old bread, crusts removed, cut into chunks (or 1 1/2 cups bread crumbs)
- 1/2 cup extra-virgin olive oil
- 1/4 cup red wine vinegar (or white wine vinegar)
- 1/4 cup water (adjust for consistency)
- 1/4 cup chopped walnuts (optional, for added texture and flavor)
- Salt to taste
- 1/2 tsp black pepper (optional)

Instructions:

1. **Prepare the Bread:**
   - If using bread chunks, soak them in water for about 5 minutes, then squeeze out excess moisture. If using bread crumbs, skip this step.
2. **Combine Ingredients:**
   - In a food processor or blender, combine the soaked bread (or bread crumbs) with minced garlic. Blend until you get a smooth mixture.
3. **Add Olive Oil and Vinegar:**
   - While the food processor is running, slowly add the olive oil and red wine vinegar. Continue to blend until the mixture is creamy and smooth.
4. **Adjust Consistency:**
   - Add water a little at a time to reach your desired consistency. Skordalia can be thick or slightly more fluid, depending on preference.
5. **Season and Serve:**
   - Stir in chopped walnuts if using.
   - Season with salt and pepper to taste.
   - Transfer to a serving dish and drizzle with a little extra olive oil on top if desired.

Optional Garnish:

- Garnish with additional chopped walnuts or a sprinkle of fresh parsley if desired.

Serve Skordalia with warm pita bread, grilled vegetables, or as a dip for a variety of appetizers. Enjoy!

Htipiti (Feta and Pepper Dip)

Ingredients:

- 8 oz (225g) feta cheese, crumbled
- 1 large red bell pepper, roasted, peeled, and chopped (or 1 cup jarred roasted red peppers, drained)
- 2 cloves garlic, minced
- 1/4 cup extra-virgin olive oil
- 1 tbsp lemon juice
- 1/2 tsp dried oregano
- Salt and black pepper to taste
- Fresh parsley or dill, chopped (optional, for garnish)

Instructions:

1. **Prepare the Peppers:**
   - If using fresh peppers, roast them over an open flame or in the oven until the skin is charred. Place them in a bowl covered with plastic wrap for 10 minutes, then peel off the skin, remove seeds, and chop. If using jarred peppers, simply drain and chop.
2. **Blend the Ingredients:**
   - In a food processor or blender, combine crumbled feta cheese, roasted red peppers, minced garlic, olive oil, lemon juice, and oregano. Blend until smooth.
3. **Season and Adjust:**
   - Taste and adjust seasoning with salt and black pepper as needed. If the dip is too thick, add a little more olive oil or a splash of water to reach the desired consistency.
4. **Serve:**
   - Transfer the dip to a serving bowl. Garnish with chopped parsley or dill if desired.

Enjoy Htipiti with pita bread, fresh vegetables, or as a spread for sandwiches and wraps!

Kokkinisto (Beef in Tomato Sauce)

Ingredients:

- 2 lbs (900g) beef stew meat, cut into chunks
- 1/4 cup olive oil
- 2 large onions, chopped
- 4 cloves garlic, minced
- 1 can (14 oz) crushed tomatoes
- 1/4 cup tomato paste
- 1 cup red wine (optional)
- 1 cup beef broth
- 2 bay leaves
- 1 tsp dried oregano
- 1/2 tsp ground cinnamon
- 1/4 tsp ground cloves
- Salt and black pepper to taste
- 1 tbsp sugar (optional, to balance acidity)

Instructions:

1. **Brown the Meat:**
   - Heat olive oil in a large pot or Dutch oven over medium-high heat.
   - Add beef chunks and brown on all sides. Remove the beef and set aside.
2. **Cook the Aromatics:**
   - In the same pot, add chopped onions and cook until softened, about 5 minutes.
   - Stir in minced garlic and cook for an additional minute.
3. **Add Tomato and Wine:**
   - Stir in tomato paste and cook for 2 minutes.
   - Add crushed tomatoes, red wine (if using), and beef broth. Stir to combine.
4. **Simmer:**
   - Return the browned beef to the pot. Add bay leaves, oregano, cinnamon, cloves, salt, and pepper. Stir well.
   - Bring to a boil, then reduce heat to low, cover, and simmer for 1.5 to 2 hours, or until the beef is tender and the sauce has thickened.
5. **Adjust Flavor:**
   - Taste and adjust seasoning with additional salt, pepper, or sugar if desired.
6. **Serve:**
   - Serve the Kokkinisto hot over rice, pasta, or with crusty bread.

Enjoy your rich and comforting Greek beef stew!

Panzaria Me Skordalia (Beetroot Salad with Garlic Dip)

Ingredients:

For the Beetroot Salad:

- 4 medium beetroots, boiled or roasted, peeled, and sliced
- 1 small red onion, thinly sliced
- 2 tbsp extra-virgin olive oil
- 1 tbsp red wine vinegar (or balsamic vinegar)
- Salt and black pepper to taste
- Fresh parsley or dill, chopped (for garnish)

For the Skordalia (Garlic Dip):

- 4-5 large garlic cloves, minced
- 2 cups day-old bread, crusts removed, cut into chunks (or 1 1/2 cups bread crumbs)
- 1/2 cup extra-virgin olive oil
- 1/4 cup red wine vinegar (or white wine vinegar)
- 1/4 cup water (adjust for consistency)
- 1/4 cup chopped walnuts (optional, for added texture and flavor)
- Salt to taste
- 1/2 tsp black pepper (optional)

Instructions:

1. **Prepare the Beetroot Salad:**
   - If you haven't already, boil or roast the beetroots until tender. Let them cool, then peel and slice.
   - In a large bowl, toss the beetroot slices and red onion with olive oil and vinegar. Season with salt and black pepper to taste.
   - Garnish with chopped parsley or dill.
2. **Prepare the Skordalia:**
   - If using bread chunks, soak them in water for about 5 minutes, then squeeze out excess moisture. If using bread crumbs, skip this step.
   - In a food processor or blender, combine the soaked bread (or bread crumbs) with minced garlic. Blend until smooth.
   - While the food processor is running, slowly add the olive oil and vinegar. Continue blending until the mixture is creamy and smooth.
   - Add water a little at a time to reach your desired consistency. Skordalia can be thick or slightly more fluid, depending on preference.
   - Stir in chopped walnuts if using. Season with salt and pepper to taste.
3. **Assemble and Serve:**

- Serve the beetroot salad with a dollop of Skordalia on the side or as a topping. You can also drizzle some Skordalia over the beetroot salad.

Enjoy your refreshing and flavorful Panzaria Me Skordalia!

Revithada (Chickpea Stew)

Ingredients:

- 2 cups dried chickpeas, soaked overnight and drained (or 2 cans chickpeas, drained and rinsed)
- 1/4 cup extra-virgin olive oil
- 1 large onion, chopped
- 4 cloves garlic, minced
- 1 large carrot, chopped
- 2 large tomatoes, diced (or 1 can diced tomatoes)
- 1/4 cup tomato paste
- 1 cup vegetable or chicken broth
- 1 tsp dried oregano
- 1/2 tsp ground cumin
- 1/2 tsp ground paprika
- 1 bay leaf
- Salt and black pepper to taste
- Fresh parsley, chopped (for garnish)

Instructions:

1. **Prepare the Chickpeas:**
    - If using dried chickpeas, soak them overnight in plenty of water. Drain and rinse before using.
    - If using canned chickpeas, simply drain and rinse them.
2. **Cook the Aromatics:**
    - Heat olive oil in a large pot over medium heat.
    - Add chopped onion and cook until softened, about 5 minutes.
    - Stir in minced garlic and cook for another minute.
3. **Add Vegetables and Spices:**
    - Add chopped carrot and cook for 5 minutes.
    - Stir in diced tomatoes, tomato paste, oregano, cumin, paprika, and bay leaf. Cook for 2 minutes, allowing the tomato paste to caramelize slightly.
4. **Add Chickpeas and Broth:**
    - Add the soaked chickpeas (or canned chickpeas) and vegetable or chicken broth to the pot. Stir well.
5. **Simmer:**
    - Bring to a boil, then reduce heat to low. Cover and simmer for 1-1.5 hours (if using dried chickpeas) or 30 minutes (if using canned chickpeas), or until the chickpeas are tender and the stew has thickened.
6. **Season and Serve:**
    - Remove the bay leaf and season with salt and black pepper to taste.

- Garnish with chopped fresh parsley before serving.

Enjoy your hearty and flavorful Revithada!

Lahanosalata (Cabbage Salad)

Ingredients:

- 1 small head of green cabbage, finely shredded
- 2 large carrots, peeled and grated
- 1 small red onion, thinly sliced
- 1/2 cup chopped fresh parsley
- 1/2 cup extra-virgin olive oil
- 2 tbsp red wine vinegar (or white wine vinegar)
- 1 tsp Dijon mustard
- 1 tsp honey (optional, for a touch of sweetness)
- Salt and black pepper to taste
- 1/4 cup sliced black olives (optional)
- 1/4 cup crumbled feta cheese (optional)

Instructions:

1. **Prepare the Vegetables:**
    - In a large bowl, combine the shredded cabbage, grated carrots, sliced red onion, and chopped parsley.
2. **Make the Dressing:**
    - In a small bowl, whisk together olive oil, red wine vinegar, Dijon mustard, and honey (if using). Season with salt and black pepper to taste.
3. **Combine and Toss:**
    - Pour the dressing over the cabbage mixture. Toss well to coat all the vegetables evenly.
4. **Optional Additions:**
    - If desired, add sliced black olives and crumbled feta cheese to the salad. Toss gently to combine.
5. **Chill and Serve:**
    - Allow the salad to sit for at least 30 minutes before serving to let the flavors meld together. Serve chilled or at room temperature.

Enjoy your refreshing and crunchy Lahanosalata!

Pita with Spinach and Feta

Ingredients:

- **For the Filling:**
    - 1 lb (450g) fresh spinach, washed and chopped (or 1 package frozen spinach, thawed and drained)
    - 1 cup crumbled feta cheese
    - 1/2 cup ricotta cheese
    - 1/4 cup chopped fresh dill (or 2 tbsp dried dill)
    - 1/4 cup chopped fresh parsley
    - 1 large egg, beaten
    - Salt and black pepper to taste
- **For the Assembly:**
    - 8 sheets of phyllo dough (thawed if frozen)
    - 1/2 cup melted butter or olive oil (for brushing)

Instructions:

1. **Prepare the Filling:**
    - In a large bowl, combine the chopped spinach, crumbled feta, ricotta cheese, dill, parsley, and beaten egg. Mix well. Season with salt and black pepper to taste.
2. **Assemble the Pita:**
    - Preheat your oven to 375°F (190°C) and grease a baking dish (about 9x13 inches).
    - Lay one sheet of phyllo dough in the baking dish and brush lightly with melted butter or olive oil. Repeat with 4 more sheets, layering them and brushing each with butter or oil.
    - Spread the spinach and feta mixture evenly over the layered phyllo dough.
    - Top with the remaining 4 sheets of phyllo dough, brushing each sheet with butter or oil as before.
3. **Bake:**
    - Using a sharp knife, cut the pita into squares or diamonds before baking to make it easier to serve.
    - Bake in the preheated oven for 30-35 minutes, or until the top is golden brown and crispy.
4. **Cool and Serve:**
    - Allow the pita to cool slightly before cutting into pieces and serving.

Enjoy your delicious Tiropita warm or at room temperature!

Feta Saganaki

Ingredients:

- 8 oz (225g) block of feta cheese
- 1/2 cup all-purpose flour
- 1/4 cup olive oil
- 1/2 tsp dried oregano
- Freshly ground black pepper to taste
- Lemon wedges, for serving
- Fresh parsley, chopped (optional, for garnish)

Instructions:

1. **Prepare the Feta:**
   - Slice the feta cheese block into thick slices, about 1/2 inch thick.
2. **Coat the Feta:**
   - Place the flour in a shallow dish.
   - Dredge each slice of feta in the flour, shaking off any excess. Make sure the feta slices are evenly coated.
3. **Heat the Oil:**
   - Heat the olive oil in a large skillet over medium-high heat.
4. **Fry the Feta:**
   - Add the floured feta slices to the skillet and cook for 2-3 minutes per side, or until golden brown and crispy. Be careful not to overcrowd the pan; cook in batches if necessary.
5. **Season and Serve:**
   - Remove the feta from the skillet and place on a paper towel-lined plate to drain any excess oil.
   - Sprinkle with dried oregano and freshly ground black pepper.
   - Serve immediately with lemon wedges for squeezing over the top. Garnish with fresh parsley if desired.

Enjoy your delicious and crispy Feta Saganaki as an appetizer or part of a Greek mezze platter!

Megalokavourmas (Big Pork Roast)

Ingredients:

- 5-6 lbs (2.3-2.7 kg) pork shoulder or pork butt
- 1/4 cup olive oil
- 6 cloves garlic, minced
- 2 tbsp dried oregano
- 1 tbsp dried thyme
- 1 tbsp paprika
- 1 tsp ground cumin
- 1 tsp ground coriander
- 1/2 tsp ground cinnamon
- 1/4 tsp ground cloves
- Salt and black pepper to taste
- 1 cup white wine or chicken broth
- 1/4 cup red wine vinegar
- 2 bay leaves
- Fresh parsley, chopped (optional, for garnish)

Instructions:

1. **Prepare the Marinade:**
    - In a small bowl, mix olive oil, minced garlic, oregano, thyme, paprika, cumin, coriander, cinnamon, cloves, salt, and black pepper.
2. **Season the Pork:**
    - Rub the pork shoulder with the marinade, making sure to coat all sides. If possible, let it marinate in the refrigerator for at least 2 hours or overnight for better flavor.
3. **Preheat the Oven:**
    - Preheat your oven to 325°F (160°C).
4. **Roast the Pork:**
    - Place the marinated pork in a large roasting pan. Pour the white wine or chicken broth and red wine vinegar around the pork.
    - Add bay leaves to the pan.
    - Cover the roasting pan with foil.
5. **Cook:**
    - Roast in the preheated oven for about 4 to 5 hours, or until the pork is tender and can be easily shredded with a fork. Baste occasionally with the pan juices.
6. **Crisp the Exterior (Optional):**
    - For a crispy exterior, remove the foil during the last 30 minutes of cooking and increase the oven temperature to 375°F (190°C).
7. **Rest and Serve:**

- Remove the pork from the oven and let it rest for 15-20 minutes before slicing.
- Garnish with chopped fresh parsley if desired.

Enjoy your flavorful Megalokavourmas with roasted vegetables or as part of a festive meal!

Bougatsa (Custard Pie)

Ingredients:

For the Custard Filling:

- 4 cups milk
- 1 cup granulated sugar
- 1/2 cup cornstarch
- 4 large egg yolks
- 1 tsp vanilla extract
- 1/4 tsp ground cinnamon (optional)

For the Assembly:

- 1 package phyllo dough (16 oz), thawed
- 1/2 cup unsalted butter, melted (or you can use vegetable oil)
- Powdered sugar (for dusting)
- Ground cinnamon (for dusting, optional)

Instructions:

1. **Prepare the Custard Filling:**
    - In a medium saucepan, heat the milk over medium heat until it is hot but not boiling.
    - In a bowl, whisk together the sugar and cornstarch. Gradually add this mixture to the hot milk, whisking continuously.
    - Cook over medium heat, whisking constantly, until the mixture thickens and begins to bubble.
    - Remove from heat and whisk in the egg yolks one at a time. Continue to whisk until smooth.
    - Return to the heat and cook for another 1-2 minutes, or until the custard is thickened to a pudding-like consistency.
    - Remove from heat and stir in vanilla extract. Let the custard cool slightly.
2. **Assemble the Bougatsa:**
    - Preheat your oven to 350°F (175°C). Grease a 9x13-inch baking dish.
    - Place one sheet of phyllo dough in the greased baking dish and brush lightly with melted butter. Repeat with 6-8 more sheets, brushing each sheet with butter.
    - Spread the custard filling evenly over the layered phyllo dough.
    - Cover the custard with 6-8 more sheets of phyllo, again brushing each sheet with melted butter.
    - Tuck in the edges of the phyllo dough around the custard to seal it.
3. **Bake:**

- Bake in the preheated oven for 30-35 minutes, or until the phyllo is golden brown and crispy.
4. **Cool and Serve:**
    - Allow the Bougatsa to cool completely before cutting into squares.
    - Dust with powdered sugar and ground cinnamon before serving if desired.

Enjoy your delicious and creamy Bougatsa!

Mizithra Cheese Pasta

Ingredients:

- 12 oz (340g) pasta (such as spaghetti, fettuccine, or penne)
- 1/4 cup unsalted butter
- 1 cup Mizithra cheese, grated (or ricotta salata as a substitute)
- 1/2 cup grated Parmesan cheese
- 2 cloves garlic, minced
- 1/4 cup fresh parsley, chopped (optional, for garnish)
- Salt and freshly ground black pepper to taste
- Lemon zest (optional, for garnish)

Instructions:

1. **Cook the Pasta:**
   - Bring a large pot of salted water to a boil. Cook the pasta according to the package instructions until al dente.
   - Reserve 1/2 cup of pasta water, then drain the pasta and set aside.
2. **Prepare the Sauce:**
   - In a large skillet, melt the butter over medium heat.
   - Add the minced garlic and cook for about 1-2 minutes, or until fragrant and lightly golden. Be careful not to let it burn.
3. **Combine Pasta and Sauce:**
   - Add the drained pasta to the skillet with the garlic and butter. Toss to coat the pasta evenly.
   - Gradually add the grated Mizithra cheese and Parmesan cheese, tossing constantly until the cheeses melt and coat the pasta. If the sauce seems too thick, add a bit of the reserved pasta water to achieve a creamy consistency.
4. **Season:**
   - Season with salt and freshly ground black pepper to taste.
5. **Garnish and Serve:**
   - Stir in the chopped parsley, if using.
   - Optionally, garnish with a bit of lemon zest for a fresh touch.
   - Serve immediately with additional Mizithra cheese on top if desired.

Enjoy your creamy, cheese-laden Mizithra Cheese Pasta!

Yemista (Stuffed Tomatoes and Peppers)

Ingredients:

For the Filling:

- 1/2 cup olive oil
- 1 large onion, finely chopped
- 2 cloves garlic, minced
- 1 cup short-grain rice (such as Arborio or Basmati)
- 1 cup canned diced tomatoes (or 2 fresh tomatoes, diced)
- 1/4 cup tomato paste
- 1/2 cup pine nuts (optional)
- 1/2 cup currants or raisins (optional)
- 1/2 cup fresh parsley, chopped
- 1/4 cup fresh dill, chopped (or 2 tbsp dried dill)
- 1 tsp dried oregano
- 1/2 tsp ground cinnamon
- Salt and black pepper to taste

For the Vegetables:

- 4 large tomatoes
- 4 large bell peppers (any color)
- Olive oil for drizzling

Instructions:

1. **Prepare the Vegetables:**
    - Preheat your oven to 375°F (190°C).
    - Cut the tops off the tomatoes and bell peppers, and carefully scoop out the seeds and insides, leaving a sturdy shell. Reserve the tops of the tomatoes.
2. **Prepare the Filling:**
    - Heat olive oil in a large skillet over medium heat.
    - Add the chopped onion and cook until softened, about 5 minutes.
    - Stir in the minced garlic and cook for another minute.
    - Add the rice and cook for 2 minutes, stirring frequently.
    - Mix in the diced tomatoes, tomato paste, pine nuts (if using), and currants or raisins (if using).
    - Stir in the parsley, dill, oregano, cinnamon, salt, and black pepper.
    - Cook for about 5 minutes, until the mixture is well combined and the rice is slightly toasted. The filling should be somewhat undercooked as it will cook further in the oven.
3. **Stuff the Vegetables:**

- Spoon the rice mixture into the hollowed-out tomatoes and bell peppers, packing the filling gently but firmly.
- Place the stuffed vegetables in a baking dish. Drizzle with olive oil and place the reserved tomato tops on the tomatoes.

4. **Bake:**
   - Cover the baking dish with foil and bake in the preheated oven for 45 minutes.
   - Remove the foil and bake for an additional 15-20 minutes, or until the vegetables are tender and the filling is cooked through.
5. **Serve:**
   - Allow the yemista to cool slightly before serving.

Enjoy your delicious and hearty Greek stuffed tomatoes and peppers!

Soutzouk Loukoum

Ingredients:

For the Syrup:

- 2 cups granulated sugar
- 1 cup water
- 1/2 cup light corn syrup
- 1/2 tsp lemon juice

For the Turkish Delight:

- 1 cup water
- 1 cup granulated sugar
- 1/2 cup cornstarch
- 1/4 tsp cream of tartar
- 1/4 cup rose water or orange blossom water (optional, for flavor)
- 1 cup chopped nuts (such as walnuts, pistachios, or almonds)
- 1/2 cup powdered sugar (for dusting)
- 1/2 cup cornstarch (for dusting)

Instructions:

1. **Prepare the Syrup:**
    - In a medium saucepan, combine granulated sugar, water, light corn syrup, and lemon juice.
    - Bring to a boil over medium heat, stirring constantly until the sugar is completely dissolved.
    - Reduce the heat and let the syrup simmer for 10-15 minutes, or until it reaches a temperature of 240°F (115°C) on a candy thermometer. Remove from heat and let it cool slightly.
2. **Prepare the Turkish Delight Base:**
    - In a separate bowl, combine 1 cup water with 1/2 cup cornstarch and stir until smooth.
    - Pour the mixture into a large saucepan and cook over medium heat, stirring constantly.
    - Add the sugar gradually while continuing to stir. Add the cream of tartar.
    - Cook the mixture, stirring frequently, until it thickens and becomes translucent (about 20-30 minutes).
3. **Combine with Syrup:**
    - Slowly pour the warm syrup into the thickened cornstarch mixture, stirring continuously.

- Continue to cook over low heat for an additional 10-15 minutes, stirring constantly, until the mixture becomes thick and pulls away from the sides of the pan.

4. **Add Nuts and Flavor:**
   - Stir in the chopped nuts and rose water or orange blossom water (if using).
   - Pour the mixture into a greased 9x9-inch (23x23 cm) baking pan or dish, smoothing the top with a spatula.

5. **Set and Cut:**
   - Let the Turkish Delight cool to room temperature, then cover with plastic wrap and let it set for at least 4-6 hours or overnight.
   - Once set, dust a cutting board with a mixture of powdered sugar and cornstarch.
   - Turn the Turkish Delight out onto the dusted board and cut into small squares or pieces. Dust all sides with the powdered sugar and cornstarch mixture to prevent sticking.

Tips:

- Use a candy thermometer to ensure the syrup reaches the correct temperature.
- Be patient during the cooking process; stirring constantly is key to achieving the right texture.

Enjoy your homemade Soutzouk Loukoum as a sweet treat with tea or coffee!

Greek Lamb Chops

Ingredients:

- **For the Marinade:**
    - 8 lamb chops (about 1-inch thick)
    - 1/4 cup olive oil
    - 4 cloves garlic, minced
    - 2 tbsp fresh lemon juice (or 1 tbsp lemon zest)
    - 2 tbsp fresh rosemary, chopped (or 2 tsp dried rosemary)
    - 2 tbsp fresh oregano, chopped (or 2 tsp dried oregano)
    - 1 tsp dried thyme
    - Salt and freshly ground black pepper to taste
- **For Cooking:**
    - Olive oil, for grilling or searing

Instructions:

1. **Prepare the Marinade:**
    - In a small bowl, whisk together olive oil, minced garlic, lemon juice, rosemary, oregano, thyme, salt, and black pepper.
2. **Marinate the Lamb Chops:**
    - Place the lamb chops in a large resealable plastic bag or shallow dish.
    - Pour the marinade over the lamb chops, making sure each chop is well-coated.
    - Seal the bag or cover the dish, and refrigerate for at least 2 hours or overnight for best results.
3. **Prepare for Cooking:**
    - Preheat your grill to medium-high heat, or heat a grill pan or cast-iron skillet over medium-high heat.
4. **Grill or Sear the Lamb Chops:**
    - Brush the grill grates or skillet with a small amount of olive oil to prevent sticking.
    - Remove the lamb chops from the marinade and let any excess drip off.
    - Grill or sear the lamb chops for about 3-4 minutes per side for medium-rare, or until they reach your desired level of doneness. The internal temperature should be about 130°F (54°C) for medium-rare.
    - For a nice sear, press the lamb chops down firmly onto the grill or skillet.
5. **Rest and Serve:**
    - Transfer the cooked lamb chops to a plate and let them rest for 5 minutes before serving. This allows the juices to redistribute.
    - Garnish with additional fresh herbs and a wedge of lemon if desired.

Serving Suggestions:

- Serve the Greek lamb chops with a side of **Tzatziki** (Greek yogurt and cucumber dip), a fresh **Greek Salad**, or **Briam** (Greek roasted vegetables).
- For a complete Greek meal, consider serving with **Pita Bread** and **Hummus**.

Enjoy your flavorful and succulent Greek lamb chops!

Baked Feta with Olives and Herbs

Ingredients:

- 1 block (about 8 oz / 225g) of feta cheese
- 1/2 cup pitted olives (such as Kalamata or green olives), halved
- 2-3 tbsp olive oil
- 1-2 cloves garlic, thinly sliced
- 1 tsp dried oregano (or 1 tbsp fresh oregano, chopped)
- 1 tsp dried thyme (or 1 tbsp fresh thyme, chopped)
- 1/2 tsp red pepper flakes (optional, for a bit of heat)
- Freshly ground black pepper, to taste
- Fresh parsley or basil, chopped (for garnish)
- Lemon wedges (optional, for serving)

Instructions:

1. **Preheat Oven:**
   - Preheat your oven to 375°F (190°C).
2. **Prepare the Baking Dish:**
   - Place the block of feta cheese in a small baking dish or ovenproof skillet.
3. **Add Olives and Herbs:**
   - Scatter the halved olives around the feta cheese.
   - Drizzle the olive oil over the feta and olives.
   - Scatter the garlic slices, dried oregano, dried thyme, and red pepper flakes (if using) over the top.
4. **Bake:**
   - Bake in the preheated oven for 20-25 minutes, or until the feta is soft and slightly golden, and the olives are warmed through.
5. **Garnish and Serve:**
   - Remove from the oven and let it cool slightly.
   - Garnish with freshly ground black pepper and chopped fresh parsley or basil.
   - Serve with lemon wedges on the side, if desired.

Serving Suggestions:

- Serve the baked feta with warm **pita bread**, **crusty baguette**, or **grilled vegetables** for dipping.
- It can also be served as part of a Mediterranean meze platter, alongside items like **hummus**, **tzatziki**, and **stuffed grape leaves**.

Enjoy this savory and flavorful baked feta as a delightful appetizer or snack!

Choriatiki (Greek Village Salad)

Ingredients:

- 4 large ripe tomatoes, cut into wedges
- 1 large cucumber, peeled (optional) and sliced
- 1/2 red onion, thinly sliced
- 1/2 cup Kalamata olives, pitted
- 1/2 cup feta cheese, crumbled or in large chunks
- 1/4 cup extra-virgin olive oil
- 2 tbsp red wine vinegar
- 1 tsp dried oregano
- Salt and freshly ground black pepper to taste
- Fresh parsley or basil for garnish (optional)

Instructions:

1. **Prepare the Vegetables:**
   - Cut the tomatoes into wedges and place them in a large salad bowl.
   - Slice the cucumber and add it to the bowl.
   - Thinly slice the red onion and add it to the bowl as well.
2. **Add the Olives and Feta:**
   - Add the Kalamata olives to the bowl.
   - Crumble or place the feta cheese on top of the salad.
3. **Make the Dressing:**
   - In a small bowl or jar, whisk together the extra-virgin olive oil, red wine vinegar, and dried oregano.
   - Season with salt and freshly ground black pepper to taste. Note that the feta cheese and olives are already salty, so be cautious with the amount of additional salt.
4. **Assemble the Salad:**
   - Drizzle the dressing over the salad.
   - Gently toss the salad to combine all ingredients, being careful not to break up the feta cheese too much.
5. **Garnish and Serve:**
   - Garnish with fresh parsley or basil if desired.
   - Serve immediately or let the salad sit for a few minutes to allow the flavors to meld together.

Tips:

- For added flavor, you can include some sliced bell peppers or capers.
- This salad pairs well with grilled meats, pita bread, or as a refreshing side dish.

Enjoy your classic Greek Village Salad, a perfect blend of fresh ingredients and Mediterranean flavors!

Galaktoboureko

Ingredients:

For the Custard Filling:

- 4 cups milk
- 1 cup granulated sugar
- 1/2 cup semolina
- 4 large egg yolks
- 1 tsp vanilla extract
- 1/4 cup unsalted butter

For the Phyllo Dough:

- 1 package phyllo dough (16 oz), thawed
- 1/2 cup unsalted butter, melted (for brushing)

For the Syrup:

- 1 cup granulated sugar
- 1 cup water
- 1/2 cup honey
- 1 lemon slice
- 1 cinnamon stick

Instructions:

1. **Prepare the Custard Filling:**
    - In a large saucepan, heat the milk over medium heat until warm but not boiling.
    - In a separate bowl, mix the sugar and semolina.
    - Gradually add the sugar and semolina mixture to the warm milk, whisking constantly to avoid lumps.
    - Continue to cook over medium heat, stirring frequently, until the mixture thickens and starts to bubble.
    - Remove from heat and stir in the egg yolks one at a time. Add vanilla extract and butter, and mix until smooth.
    - Allow the custard to cool slightly.
2. **Prepare the Phyllo Dough:**
    - Preheat your oven to 350°F (175°C).
    - Brush a 9x13-inch baking dish with melted butter.
    - Lay one sheet of phyllo dough in the dish, brushing lightly with melted butter. Repeat with 7-8 more sheets, brushing each with butter.
    - Spread the custard filling evenly over the phyllo layers.

- - Cover the custard with another 7-8 sheets of phyllo dough, brushing each layer with butter. Tuck in the edges around the custard.
3. **Bake:**
   - Bake in the preheated oven for 40-45 minutes, or until the phyllo is golden brown and crispy.
4. **Prepare the Syrup:**
   - While the Galaktoboureko is baking, make the syrup. In a saucepan, combine sugar, water, honey, lemon slice, and cinnamon stick.
   - Bring to a boil over medium heat, stirring occasionally. Reduce heat and simmer for 10 minutes. Remove from heat and let it cool slightly.
5. **Finish:**
   - Once the Galaktoboureko is done baking, remove it from the oven and immediately pour the warm syrup evenly over the hot dessert.
   - Allow it to cool to room temperature before cutting into squares.

Enjoy your rich and delicious Galaktoboureko, a classic Greek dessert!